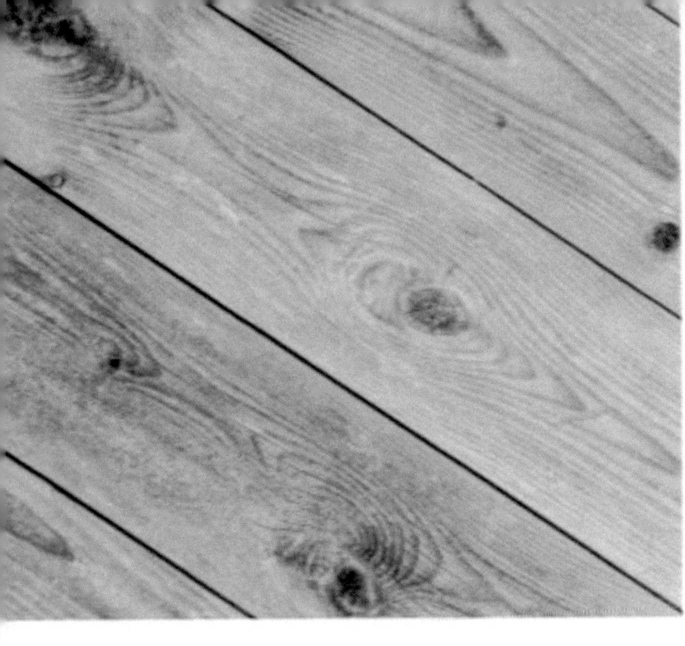

BROWN WOOD
BACKGROUND
DECORATIVE CRAFT PAPER
8 x 8 | 12 SHEETS 6 DESIGNS

CUT LUV
PAPERS

REMOVE WITH SCISSORS

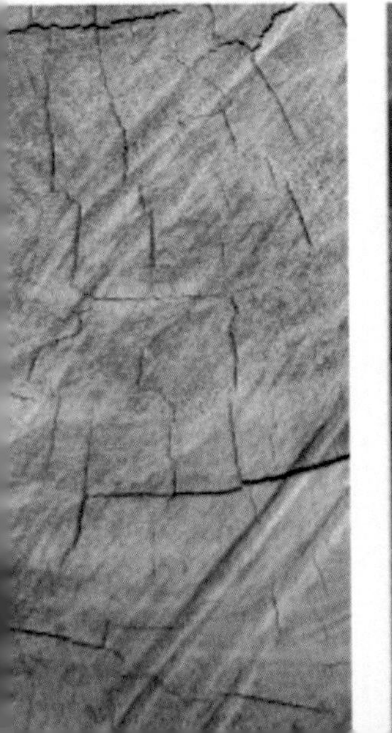
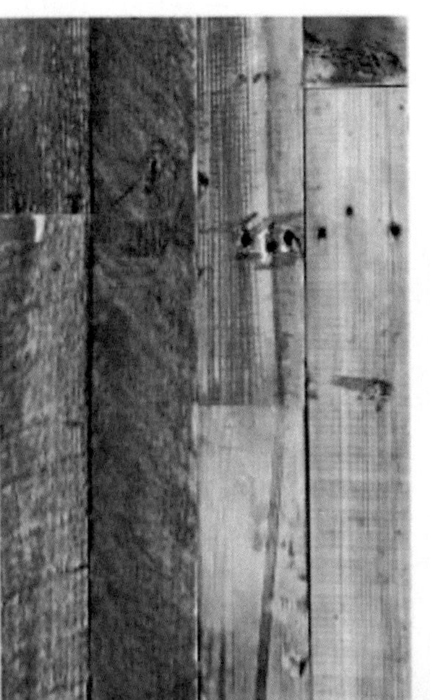
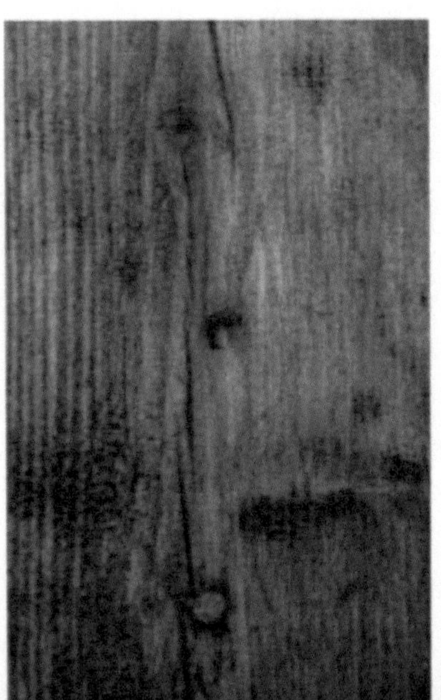
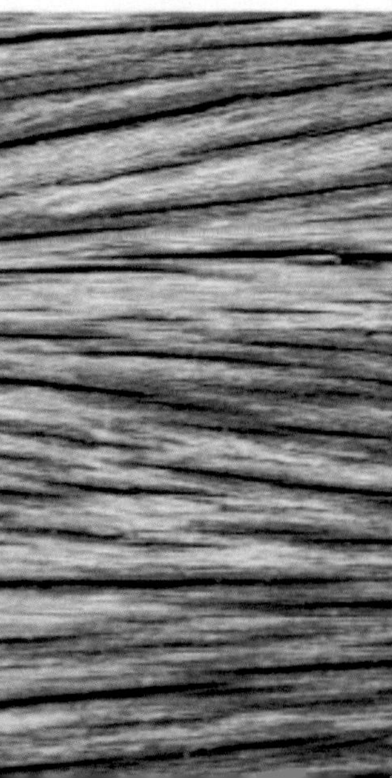

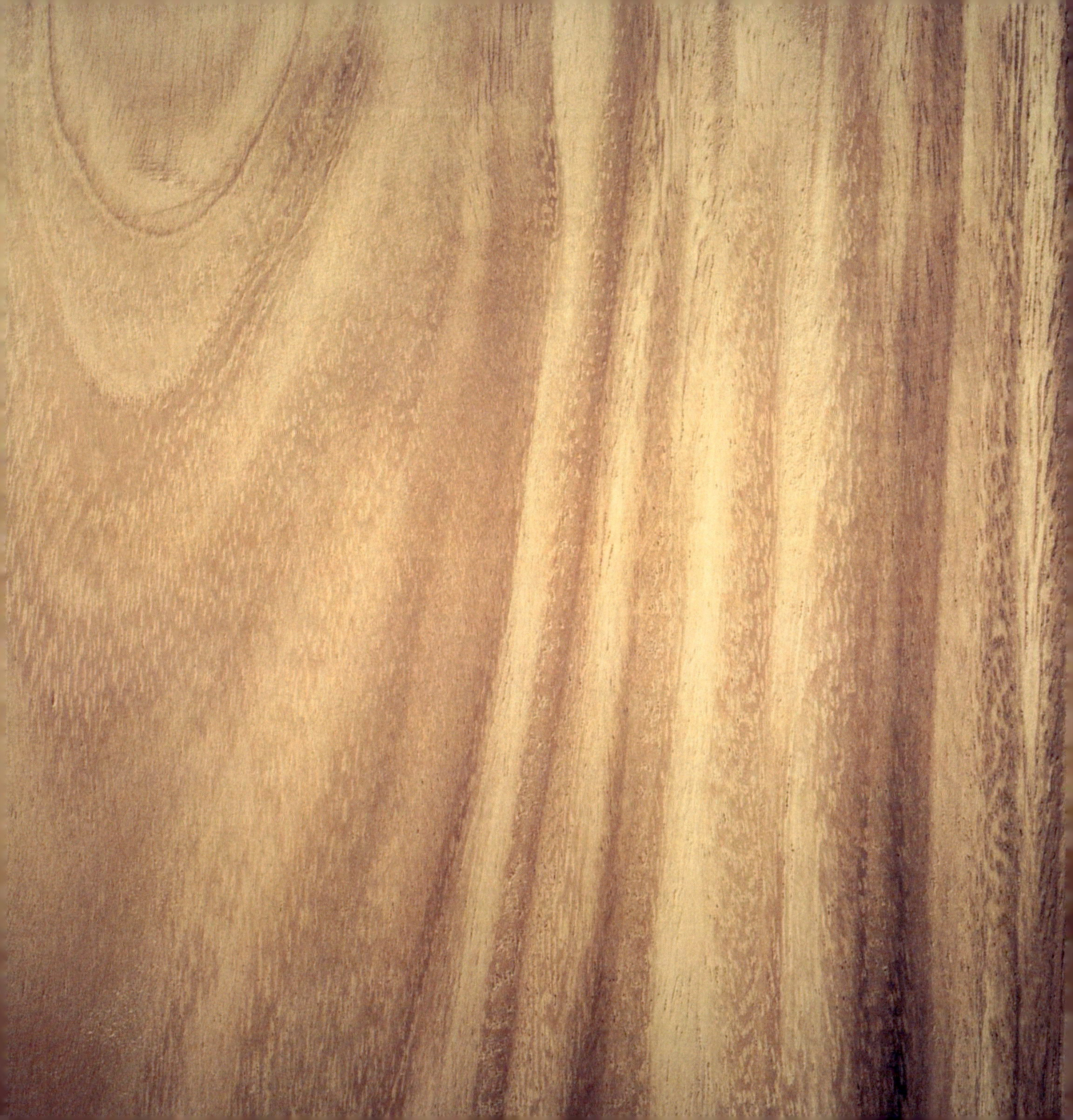

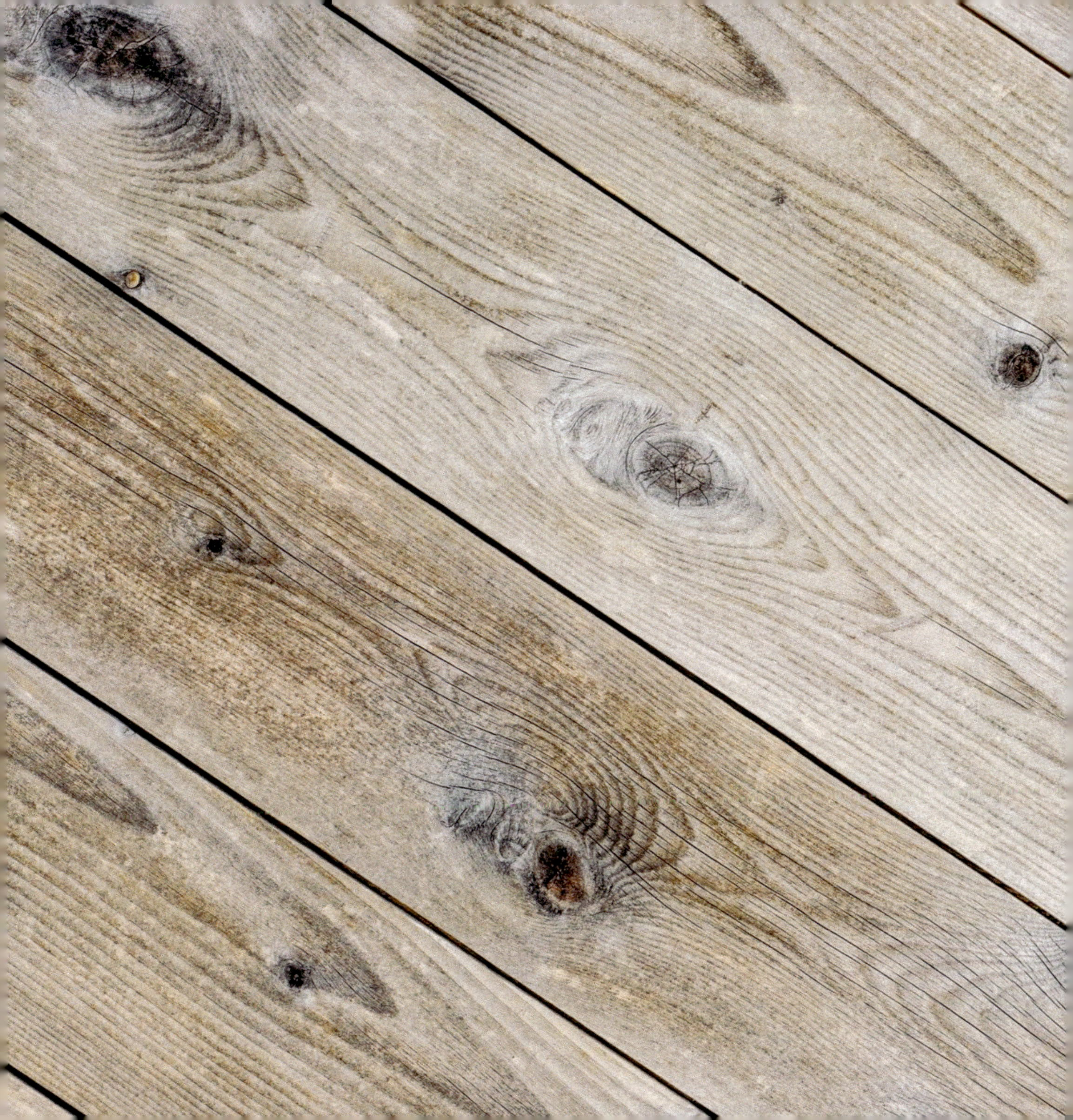

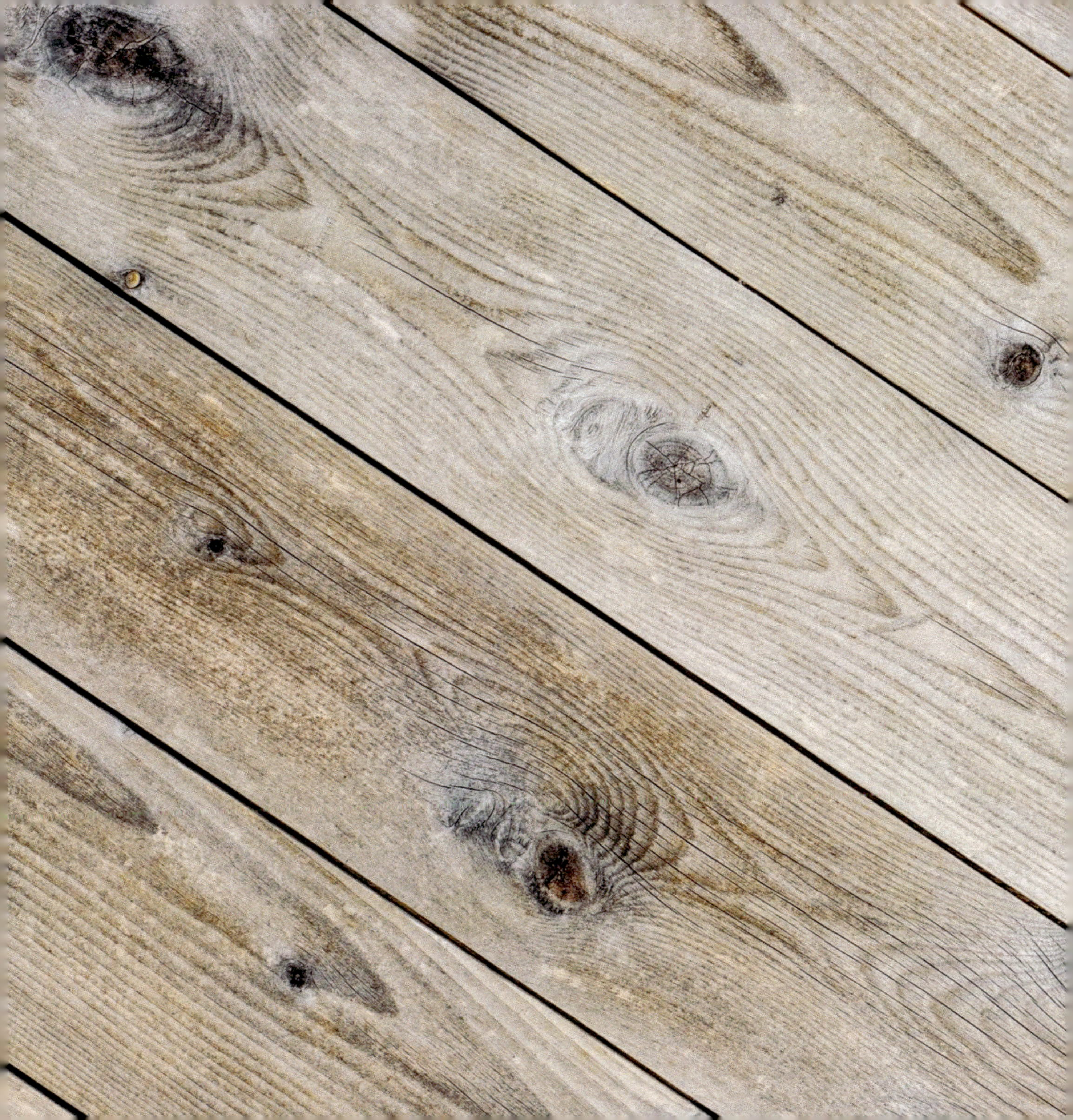

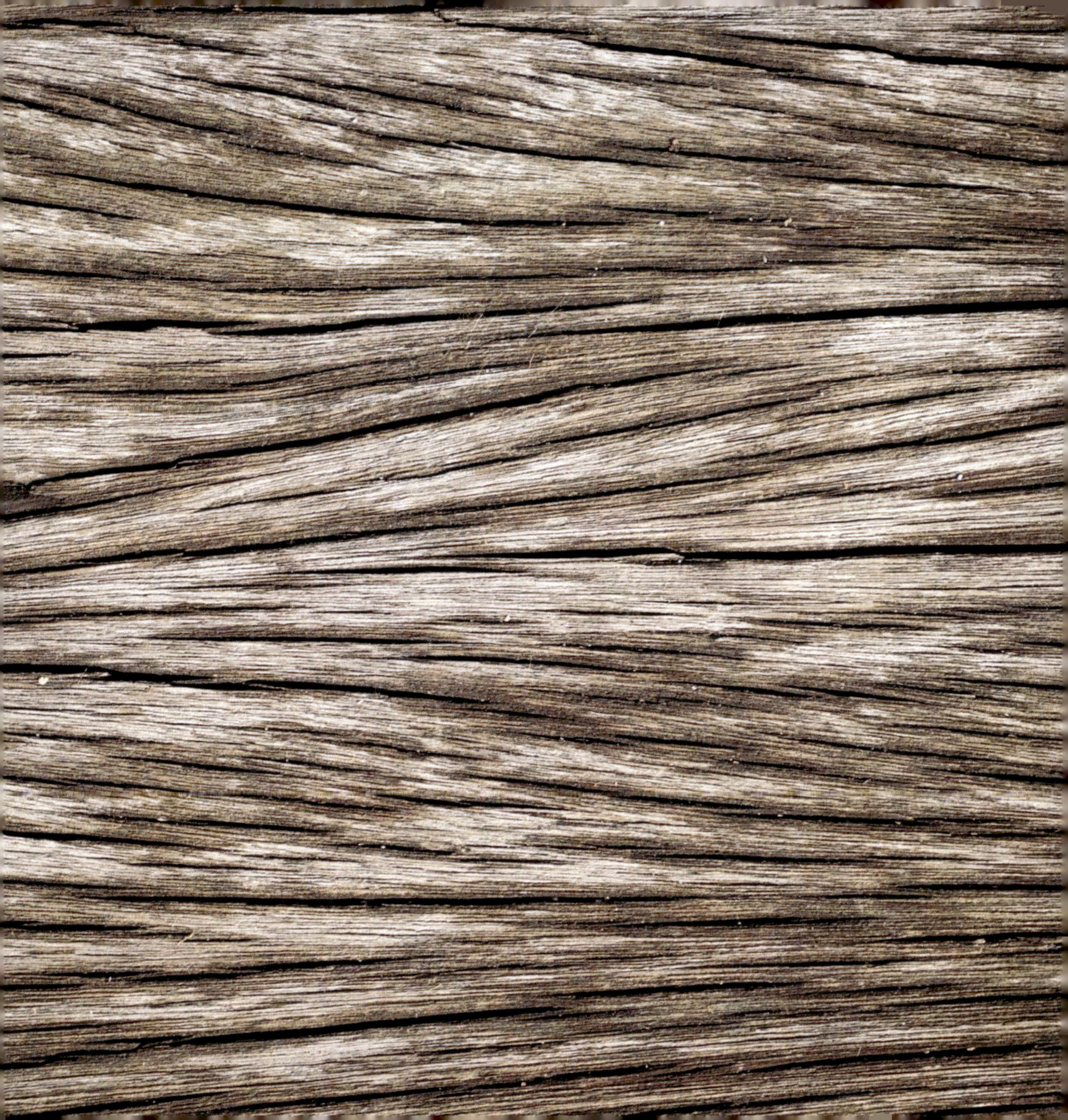

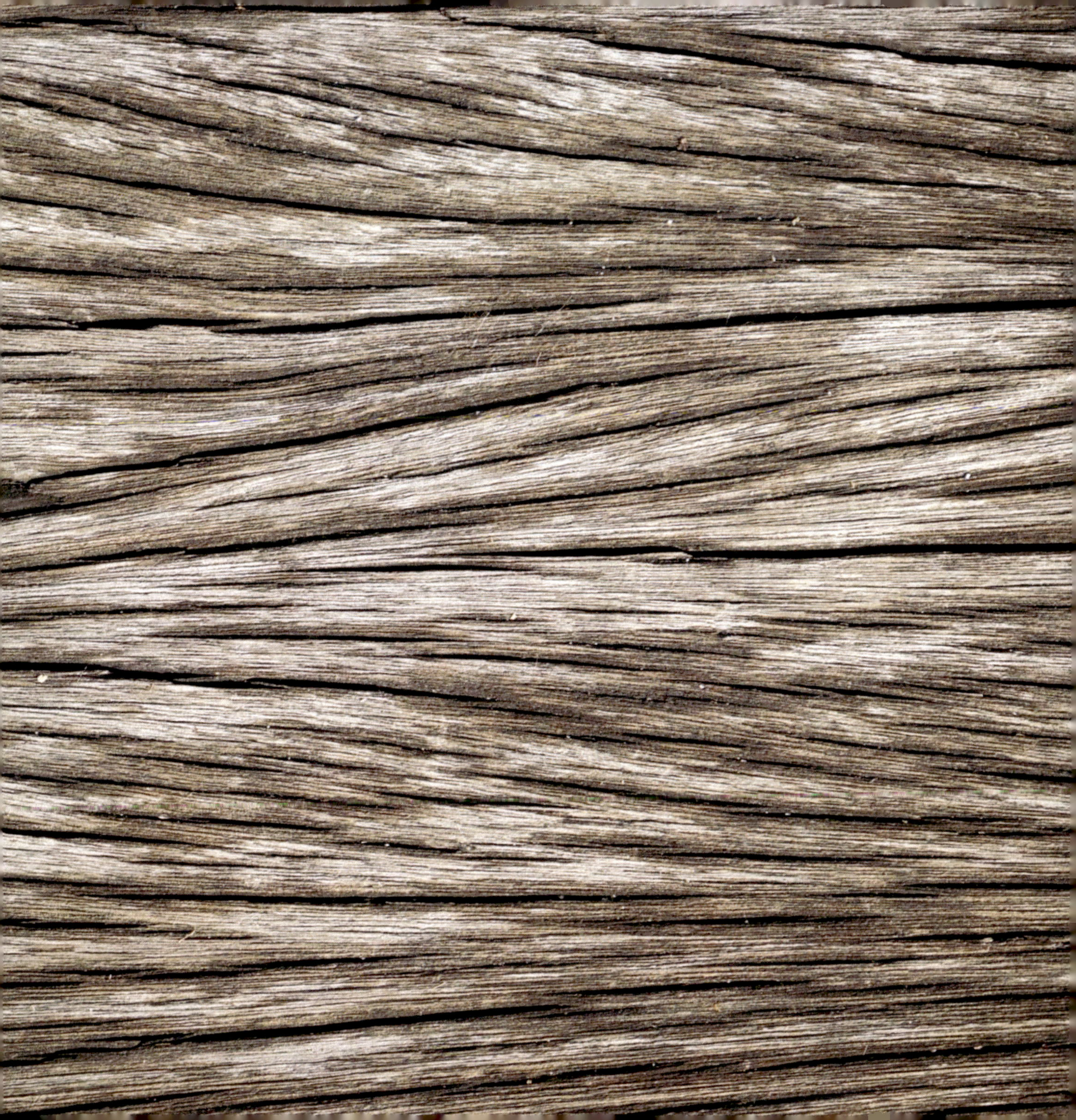

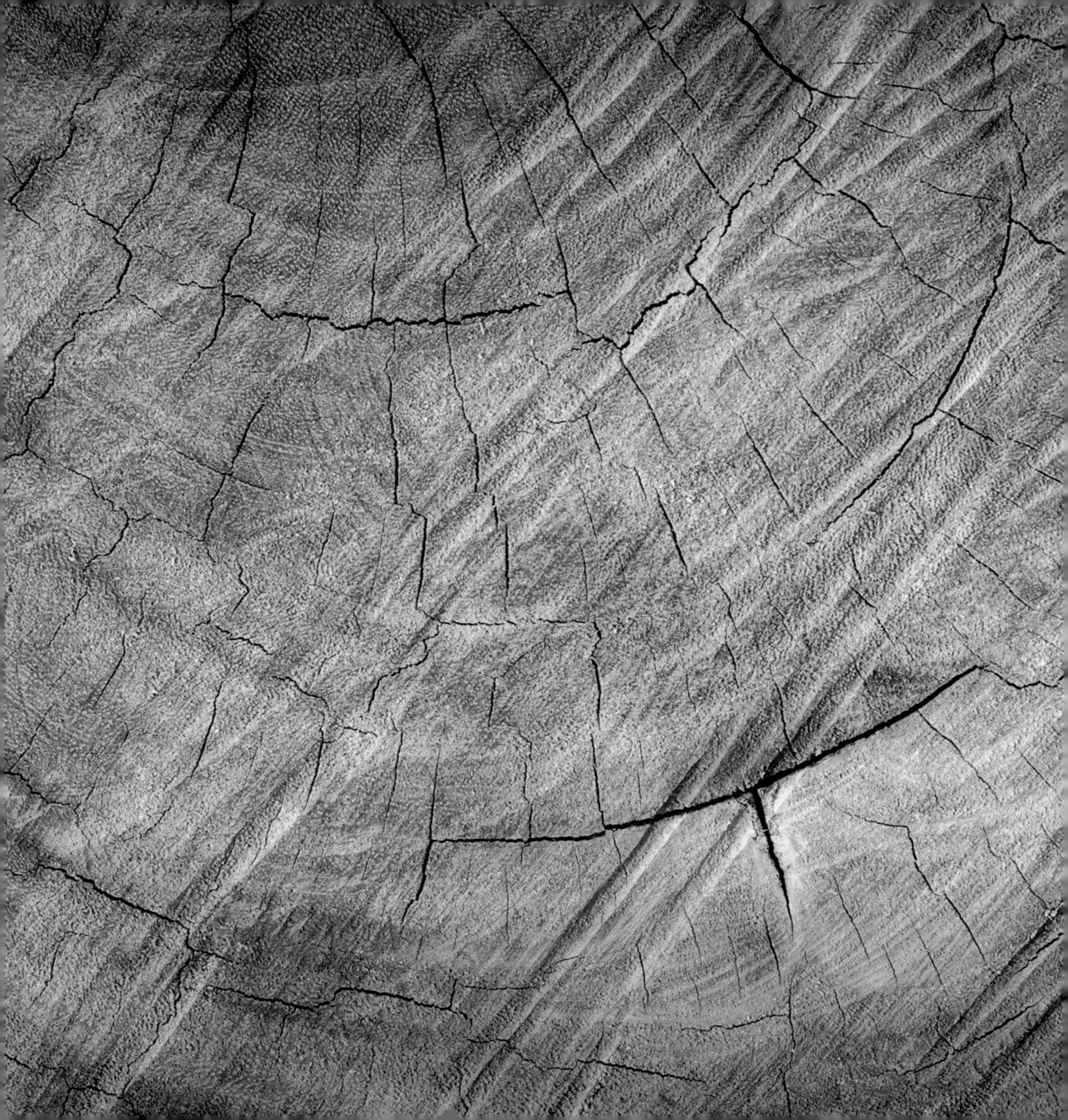

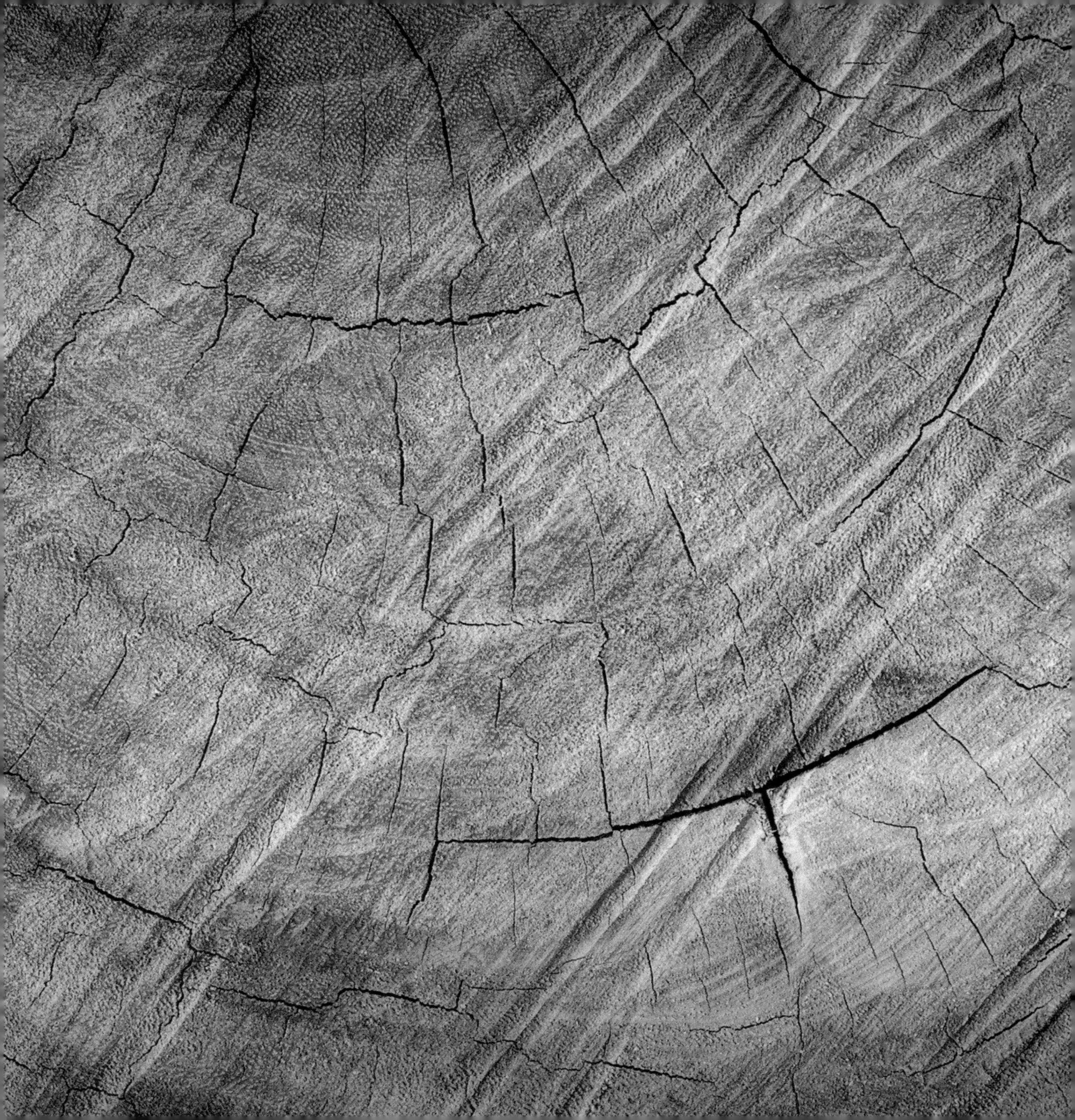

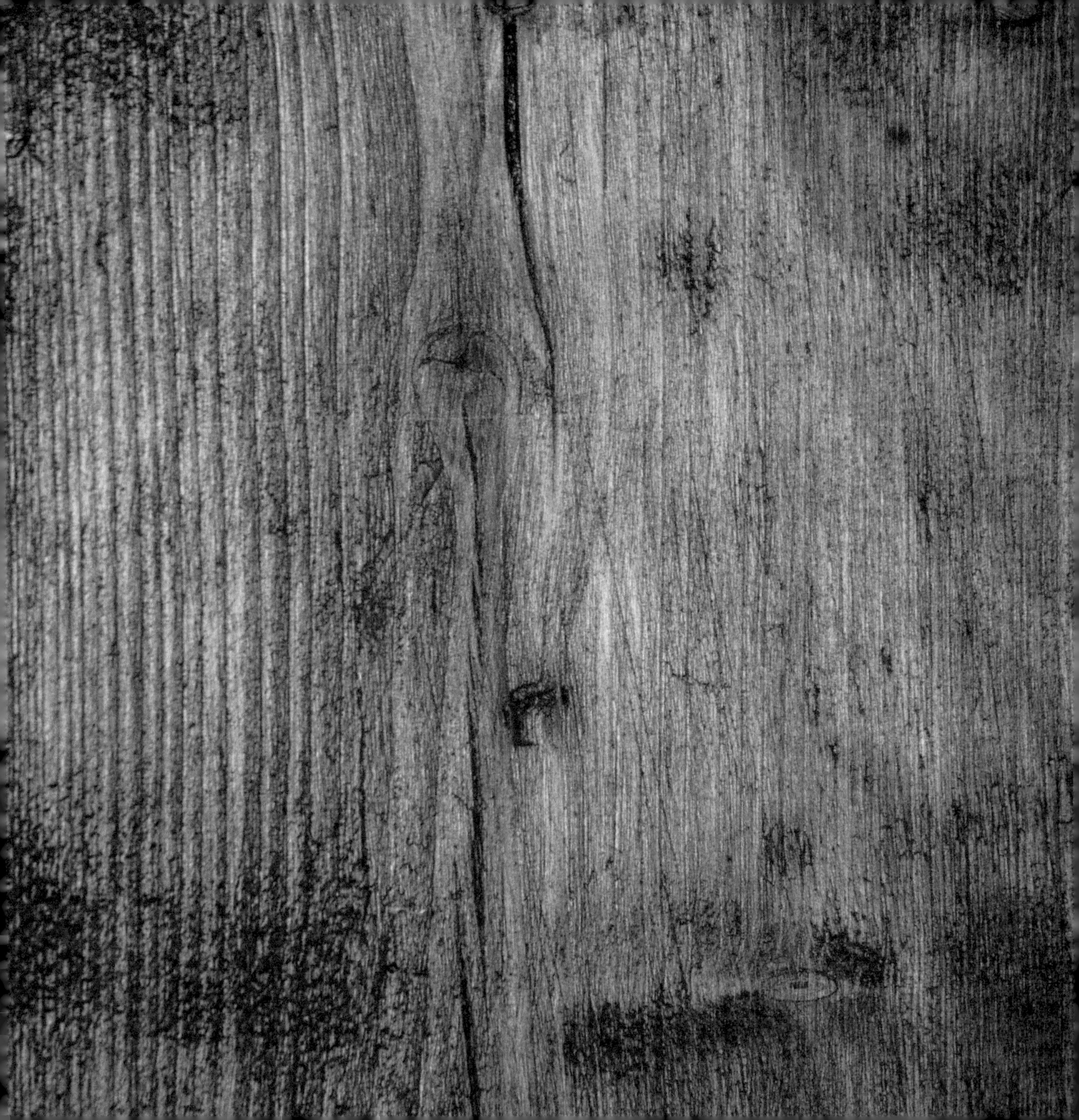

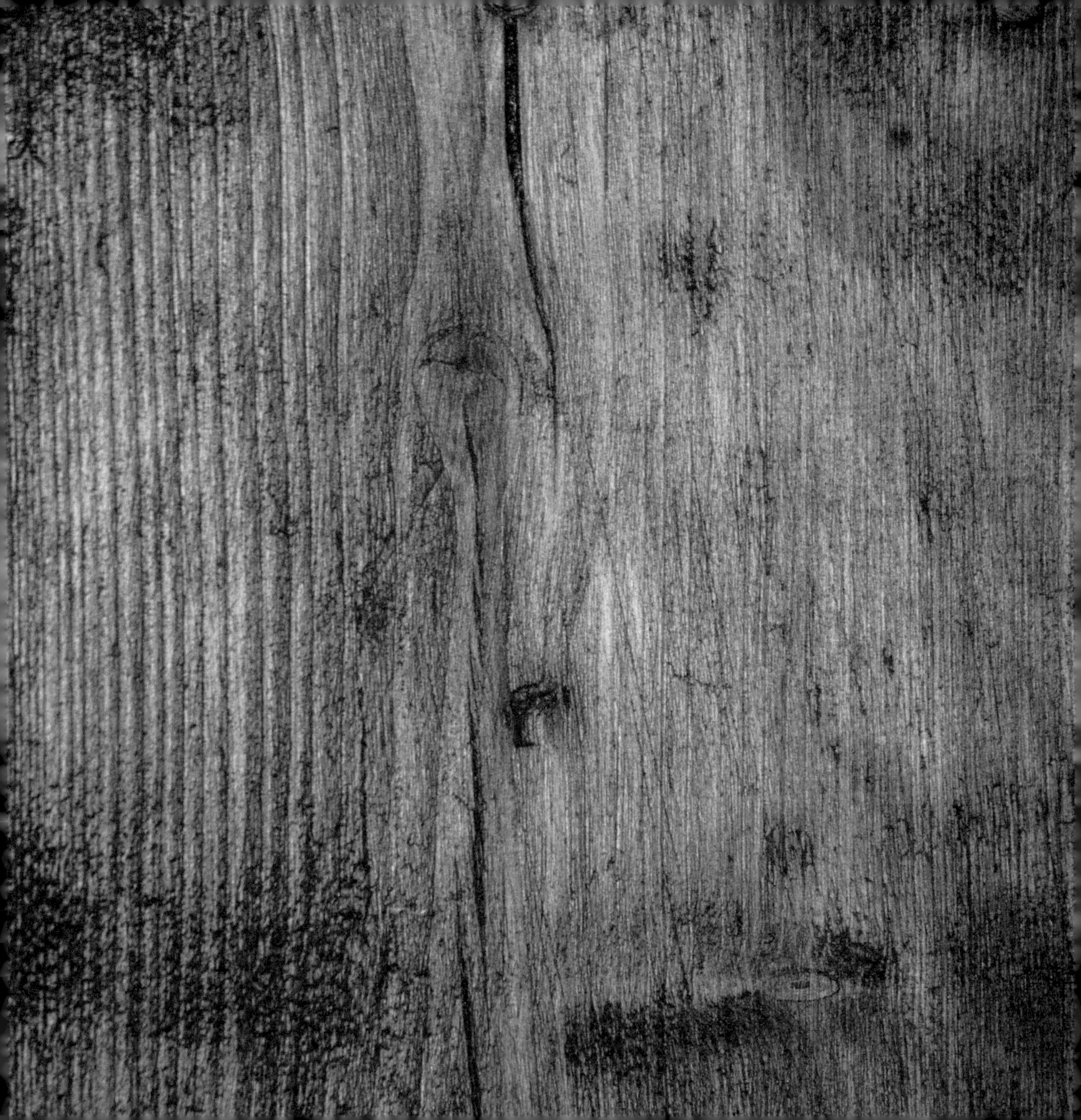

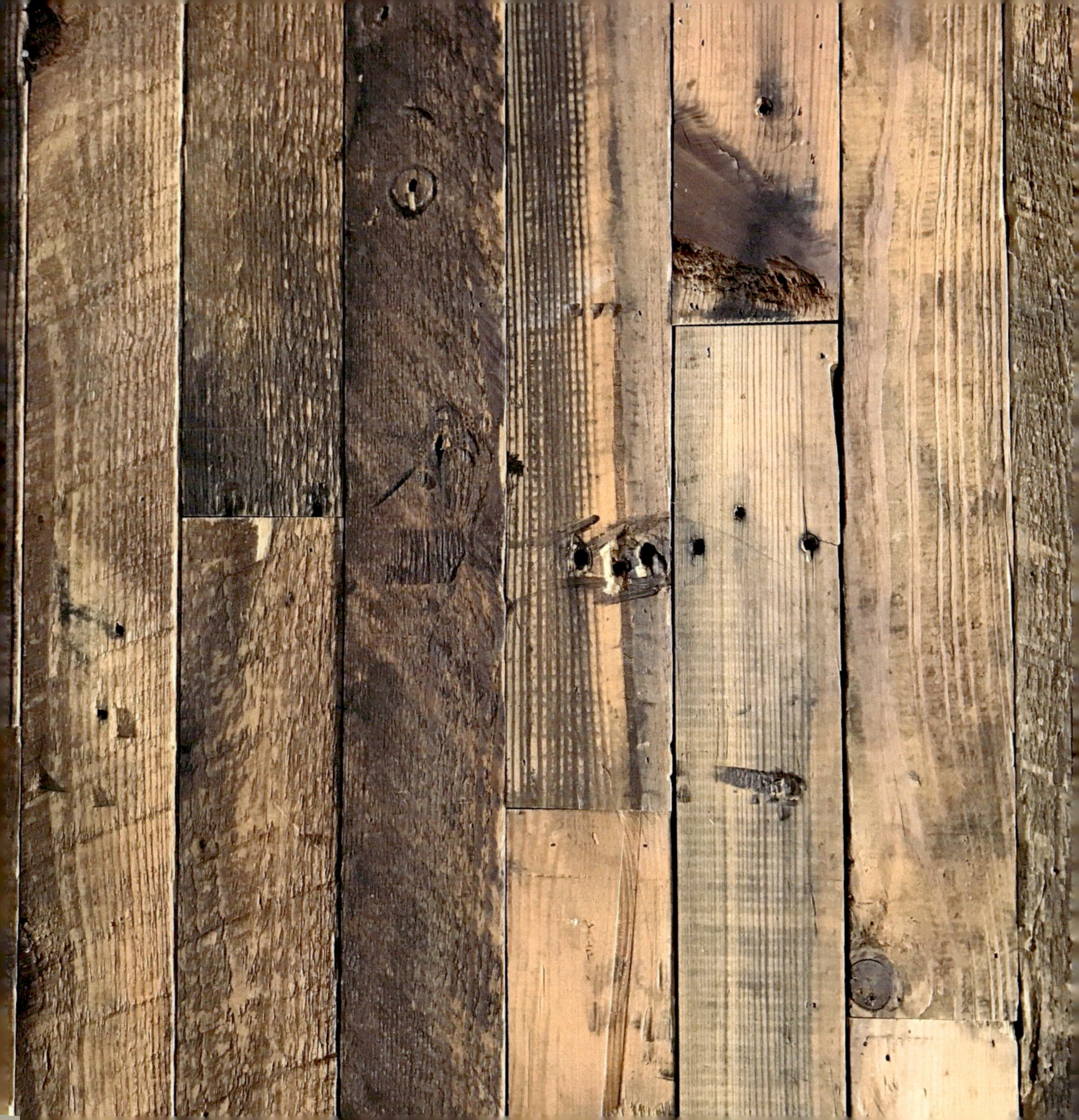

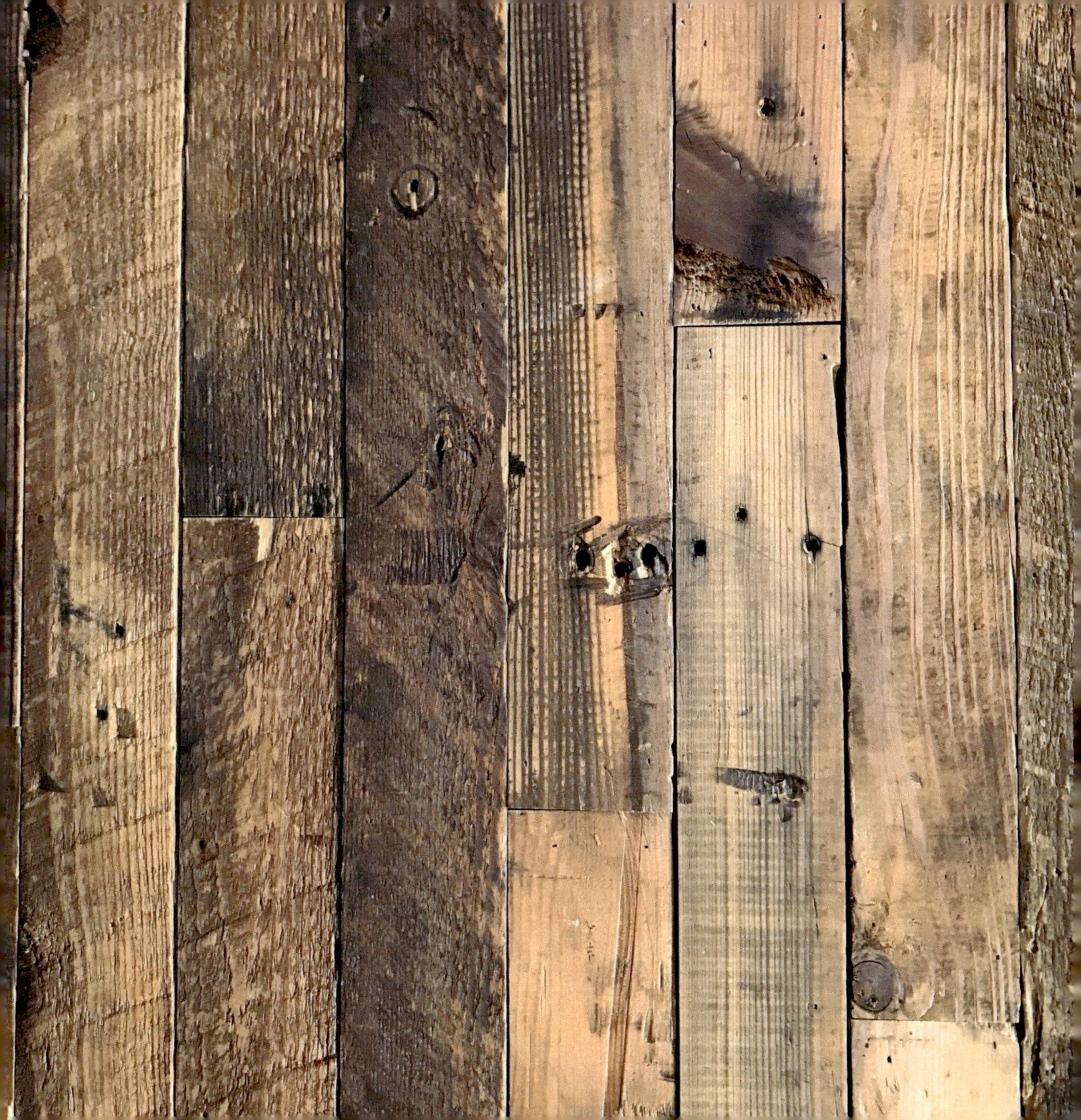

www.ingramcontent.com/pod-product-compliance
Lightning Source LLC
Chambersburg PA
CBRC091247050726
47599CB00010B/1012